AMOR APOCALYPSE

Abhijit Naskar is the twenty-first century Neuroscientist whose contributions in Cognitive and Behavioral Neuroscience have helped the world tackle the issues of systemic racism, prejudice, hate, extremism, discrimination and biases more effectively. As an untiring advocate of mental health and universal acceptance, he became a beloved best-selling author all over the world with his very first book "The Art of Neuroscience in Everything". With his pioneering ventures into the Neuropsychology of beliefs and biases, he has hugely contributed in the eradication of religious and cultural differences in our world, for which he is popularly hailed as the humanitarian scientist, who takes the human civilization in the path of sweet general harmony.

ABHIJIT
NASKAR

Lives to Serve Before I Sleep
When Humans Unite: Making A World Without Borders
All For Acceptance
Monk Meets World
Mission Reality
Citizens of Peace: Beyond The Savagery of Sovereignty
Operation Justice: To Make A Society That Needs No Law
See No Gender
The Gospel of Technology
Every Generation Needs Caretakers: The Gospel of
Patriotism
Aşkanjali: The Sufi Sermon
Mad About Humans: World Maker's Almanac
Revolution Indomable
When Call The People: My World My Responsibility
No Foreigner Only Family
Hurricane Humans: Give me accountability, I'll give you
peace
Ain't Enough to Look Human
Servitude is Sanctitude
Time To End Democracy: The Meritocratic Manifesto
I Vicdansaadet Speaking: No Rest Till The World is Lifted
Boldly Comes Justice: Sentient not Silent
Good Scientist: When Science and Service Combine
Sleepless for Society
Neden Türk: The Gospel of Secularism
Martyr Meets World: To Solve The Hard Problem of
Inhumanity
The Shape of A Human: Our America Their America
When Veins Ignite: Either Integration or Degradation
Heart Force One: Need No Gun to Defend Society
Solo Standing on Guard: Life Before Law
Generation Corazon: Nationalism is Terrorism
Mucize Insan: When The World is Family
Hometown Human: To Live For Soil and Society
Girl Over God: The Novel
Gente Mente Adelante: Prejudice Conquered is World
Conquered
Earthquakin' Egalitarian: I Die Everyday So Your Children
Can Live
Giants in Jeans: 100 Sonnets of United Earth
Vatican Virus: The Forbidden Fiction (Abi Naskar
Adventures Book 2)
Karadeniz Chronicle: The Novel (Abi Naskar Adventures

Book 3)
Şehit Sevda Society: Even in Death I Shall Live
Handcrafted Humanity: 100 Sonnets For A Blunderful
World
Mücadele Muhabbet: Gospel of An Unarmed Soldier
Making Britain Civilized: How to Gain Readmission to The
Human Race
Dervish Advaitam: Gospel of Sacred Feminines and Holy
Fathers
Honor He Wrote: 100 Sonnets For Humans Not Vegetables
The Gentalist: There's No Social Work, Only Family Work
Either Reformist or Terrorist: If You Are Terror I Am Your
Grandfather
Woman Over World: The Novel (Abi Naskar Adventures
Book 4)
High Voltage Habib: Gospel of Undoctrination
Bulldozer on Duty
Find A Cause Outside Yourself: Sermon of Sustainability
Ingan Impossible: Handbook of Hatebusting

DEDICATION

To the lovers who love beyond reward.

CONTENTS

Part 1

You know you are in love,
When the person is not a person.
More than air, water and food,
They are your life's fundamental.

You know you are in love,
Not when you wanna live with somebody,
But when you can't live without,
Their light, laughter and felicity.

Felicity of love flourishes the world,
What good is all the fear and worry!
Let all worry have me as their feast,
But my love mustn't lose their felicity.

To love is not to have them near,
To love is to wipe their tear.
Near or far, distance is delusion,
Love, till all divisions disappear.

Like a bolt from the blue love rises,
Suddenly one finds a mirror.
The beauty you find in the other,
Is what you hold in your innermost corner.

Suddenly we lose our voice,
To speak in love is blasphemy.
Declare your love without saying a word,
Either be an orator or lover on knees.

If they don't hear your silence,
Words won't do you any good.
Listen to the silence beyond the words,
And you shall hear the divine tune.

Language of love is care,
Language of love is understanding.
To bring smile on another's face,
Is what gets one smiling.

Smile has no nationality,
Smile has no exclusive identity.
A smile holds a universe within,
With it one speaks to all humanity.

The whole humanity is waiting,
It is waiting to be our family.
Then what exactly keeps us apart?
It is all our fancy exclusivity.

There's no place for exclusivity in love,
There's no place for rigidity in love.
Either we are all lost in love's sanctuary,
Or we are chained and freezing in the draught.

Cold is the world when the mind is cold,
Warmth is born of the mind made of gold.
All minds hold gold but with dust on top,
Dump the dust and lo rises, a generation of gold!

Only gold of worth comes from the heart,
All others are mere imitation.
No matter the karats on a person's body,
Without kindness all karats cause extinction.

An ounce of kindness is worth more,
Than a thousand goldmines.
Boil yourself in oil of the soil,
Till the spirit till it starts to shine.

The spirit within shines when,
All dust of narcissism subsides.
Be a lover, and labor for love,
The self expands as greed subsides.

Part 2

The wider the self gets,
The smaller the self gets.
Once the expansion starts,
Our very life is unselfed.

Better than self-help is unself-help,
To understand another is to be understood.
Better than salvation is annihilation,
To lift up another is the flight of truth.

All talk of truth is nonsense,
Be lost in love and truth comes chasing.
Truth is bosom buddy of the lover,
The rest roam hitherto without an inkling.

I am not talking about love of the surface,
For lovers of surface are destined to fall.
Scratch the surface both of yours and another,
Only then shall you be the pedestrian of dawn.

Love with your eyes, and it'll fade in a year,
Love with your horns, it'll fade even sooner.
Fall in love with the being beyond the body,
And you'll have your messy but sweet everafter.

There is no 'happily everafter',
For it implies a fictitious perfection.
All we can have is a messy togetherness,
When together, even a messy life is salvation.

All that one can hope for is to be,
Next to another as partner in mess.
When your mess and my mess combine,
We become a beacon of luminescence.

Every being is a beacon to be,
All it takes is selfless insanity.
To find life outside the self,
Is the fulfillment of our humanity.

Human chained to self is animal off the leash,
To break the chains of self is to tame the animal.
Walls are blasphemy on the ocean's universality,
Selfishness keeps the self from being universal.

There is not one self but two,
One is the image, another is potential.
Wasting all lifeforce on mere image,
One remains oblivious to the vast potential.

Self as potential is force unbound,
To bind such self is to defeat the purpose.
The eternal purpose of the self is expansion,
Without expansion all existence is hogwash.

Rigidity is drag on expansion,
For it makes chains out of roots.
Roots give ground beneath our feet,
While chains only cripple all our move.

Either rigid or alive,
You can't be both - no way!
Fall in love across fear,
It'll take your rigidity away.

If love doesn't wipe out your rigidity,
It only means your heart needs humanizing.
If rigidity is still stronger than love,
You gotta do a lot of spring cleaning.

Take our land of the free for example,
Where brutes are still run by archaic texts.
For a nation that claims to be a superpower,
We are hurtling down the course of regress.

Part 3

14

Amor Apocalypse is headed our way,
Now that Roe vs Wade is overturned.
Love is where the scrotum-brain scotus,
Will lay next their filthy hand.

First they came for our choice,
Then they'll come for our love.
Soon they'll go for good old lynching,
Land of the free will be land of the shrubs.

Straight and queer are products of a bipolar world,
In the sanctuary of love there's no straight, no queer.
In love's domain queer is straight, straight is queer,
A heart full of love and light is radiantly nonpolar.

I say this with all my humility,
To the fundamentalists particularly.
This is not meant for those of faith,
Who never claim ideological supremacy.

What do the dumbbells of bible know,
About the bold serendipities of love!
What do the captives of koran know,
About the welcoming language of the dove!

What do the vultures of vedas know,
About the elimination of assumption!
What do the militants of atheism know,
About the sweetness of assimilation!

I learnt my religion on the streets,
Like Jesus, Gautama, Shams and Shankara.
Given the choice between dogma and love,
The human always chooses love over dogma.

Love finds new meaning in every age,
Each amplifies the glory of the last one.
Those who fear expansion out of insecurity,
Deserve only pity not serious consideration.

But beware o lovers, hate not those,
Who stand as obstacle in your love.
Lovers are born to conquer hate and fear,
To reciprocate them is to dishonor love.

For every act of hate on me,
I'll give them back ten hugs.
But lay a finger on my loved ones,
I'll send them back without fingers.

This is no threat or intimidation,
I don't do threats, I am no mobster.
I am just a lover without logic,
All I can do is inform you of disaster.

If you love to fight, you are a duffer,
If you fight for love, you are a lover.
If you love to sleep, you are sober,
If you cannot sleep, you're beyond repair.

Only those who are beyond repair,
Are the ones who can fix the world.
They're insane and insensible enough,
To give up all to heal another's heart.

I'm beyond repair, beyond help,
No shallow logic can fix me.
The day I fell in love is the day,
I renounced all worldly sanity.

Sanity is poison on the fabric of love,
The sanity that world peddles is but coldness.
Such sanity has no place in civilization,
It belongs in museum next to the bones of a t-rex.

Part 4

Sanity mustn't guide life,
Life is to drive all sanity.
Sanity that undermines love,
Is the ultimate insanity.

There are two kinds of insanities,
One can be managed with medical treatment.
But the insanity that passes as the norm,
Is far worse than any clinical illness.

Handicapped is not the one with a crippled body,
Handicapped is the one with a crippled heart.
Handicap of body can be treated with prosthetics,
But there is no prosthetic for a crippled heart.

The only solution to a crippled heart is love,
If love can't make a heart walk again, nothing can.
Hence it's more important to care for heart than body,
Nourish it with good thoughts, not prehistoric junk.

A healthy belief of today may become junk tomorrow,
Belief deemed junk today may turn healthy tomorrow.
Therefore no mind should take no belief as gospel,
Every generation is to scrutinize life more and more.

To scrutinize life isn't the same as analysis,
For in life and love analysis is paralysis.
Scrutiny of life involves a simple awareness,
An awareness untainted by tradition and habits.

Tainted by tradition we've caused,
Terrible terror through centuries.
Blinded by biases we've maintained,
Nothing but unimaginable bigotry.

To measure existence of today,
By the standard of yesterday,
Is indicative of the glaring fact,
That we are going totally astray.

When are we going astray?
When are we on the right track?
Who is to decide what is rightness!
Who is to decide what's fiction, what's fact!

I have no idea who is to decide all that,
I don't have no answer for your life.
Likewise, don't take the dead as infallible,
Love them, respect them,
but don't give reins of your life.

Dead are not those who are dead in body,
Dead are those who are dead to expansion.
Uneducated are not those who are illiterate,
Uneducated are those opposed to evolution.

Education of the head achieves nothing,
If the heart remains ever so uneducated.
All the information in the world is worthless,
If they don't help you become a humanitarian aid.

Humanitarianism is a myth,
So are humanism and charity.
They are the world's way,
To sustain nothing but apathy.

Are you a devout hydrophile,
Since you drink water so well?
You are not, right - and why not!
Because water is but life's essential.

In the same way, kindness isn't an ism,
Human helping human isn't an ideology.
If they stick labels on such act of life,
It is but a sign of a rather sick society.

Part 5

26

The sun is not humanitarian,
The trees are not humanitarian.
Yet without them there is no life,
Without them all humanity is fiction.

Love like the sun,
Sing like the birds.
Do your own thing,
With love beyond rewards.

Love till you land,
Love till you fly.
Love is the land you stand,
Love is the air to life.

There is no 'my land and your land',
There is only land of love.
There is no 'my world and your world',
There is only world of love.

Better have love without land,
Than land without love.
I came, I saw, I lost myself,
Now all I am is love.

To have all but love, is to have nothing at all,
To have love but all, is to have everything.
To lose oneself in love, is to find oneself,
To seek oneself without love, is sheer fooling.

Wise is the one who knows to be fool,
Fools are those who identify as intellectual.
Lover is the one who loves without reward,
Retard are those who love and seek remuneration.

Let me tell you what is love,
What is it to be enamored in caring!
Reputation, remuneration, turn distant memory,
That is the first sign of love's awakening.

The world awakens when love awakens,
Love awakens when the human awakens.
Human awakens when humanity is prioritized,
Humanity is prioritized when all are one sentience.

When all are one sentience,
Language withers and fades away.
Let's sit together and speak in silence,
Let's be light to each other's way.

Gel, yanımda otur.
Nasıl istiyorsan, öyle olur.
İstemiyorsan konuşma, gerek yok.
Yanımdayken, sessizliğin bile sükundur.

Biliyorum, çok acıyor!
Biliyorum, bu dünya çok zalim!
Istiyorum ama soylemem - elimi tut!
Çünkü senin yaranın ilacı sadece sensin.

Senin derdin benim derdim.
Her dert insana cesaret veriyor.
Bulutlar güneş ışığının habercileridir.
Bugünün acısı yarın tacı oluyor.

Hadi gel, burada otur.
Nasıl istiyorsan, öyle olur.
Eğer konuşursan kulaklarımla dinleyeceğim.
Eğer konuşmazsan kalbimle dinleyeceğim.

Son nefesime kadar peşinden geleceğim,
Beni görsen de görmesen de.
Beni kabul edersen ya da unutursan,
Artık yaşamak seninle, ölmek seninle.

Part 6

Come, sit next to me.
As you will, so will be.
As long as you are next to me,
Even your silence is tranquility.

I know it hurts like the dickens!
Yet every wound delivers valiance.
At your every whim I am your servant.
But to every wound you are your treatment.

Your trouble is my trouble.
Be not disheartened if the world frowns.
Clouds are nothing but herald of sunshine.
Pain of today is tomorrow's crown.

So I say, come, sit next to me.
As you will, so will be.
Speak with lips or not, doesn't matter,
I'll just tune in to your heartbeat.

Till the end I'll stick by you,
Whether you acknowledge I exist.
Accept me or discard me, my dear,
I'll keep struggling for your uplift.

Love's welfare is lover's welfare,
A glint of their giggle is lover's glory.
Eyes of love are the lover's sky,
Their one hug wipes out all worry.

Those who have no love, gossip.
Lovers are too drunk to judge others.
Yet it's this drunkenness that makes a human.
Either you are drunk or gossiping duffers.

I don't discuss people,
I work on issues.
Only time I discuss a person,
Is when the person is the issue.

I am too busy to waste time discussing people,
People who can't tell suffering from inconvenience.
My people are the meek, my people are the destitute,
My people are those too hungry to pass judgment.

Find a heart that beats for others,
Find a soul that seeks for others.
Find a mind that melts for others,
And there'll be no place for petty fears.

Fear rises because we are programmed to survive,
Fear is an archetypical instinct of survival.
But all of it is programmed for a life in the jungle,
That's why most of that fear today is illogical.

Yet you can't reason with fear,
Tryna resist fear is to lose the battle.
Embrace all fear as part of you,
And they won't be able to turn you a cripple.

For those who fear reason,
No reason is enough to not fear reason.
Those who try to reason with fear,
End up only making the fear strengthened.

Fear of reason and reason with fear,
Are equally primitive and useless.
Reason only works if the mind wants to grow,
Not if it has traded growth for convenience.

Even the blind can see the light of growth,
Yet those with eyes are lost in convenience.
Even the deaf can hear the music of ascension,
Yet those with ears are lost in presumptions.

Part 7

Even a flower cannot survive in last week's water,
Yet you expect the mind to thrive that way.
Let the mind fly higher than known heights,
And all light and life will find their way.

Human brain is a time capsule of archaic instincts,
Plenty of which are actually out of place today.
Yet you can't get rid of them by flipping a switch,
You gotta overwhelm them with modern human way.

I am a very violent person,
Yet nobody has seen my violence.
I've kept it overwhelmed all my life,
With a heart full of gentleness.

I would rather be insulted and walk away,
Than let my rage get hold of me.
Because if I raise my hand at someone,
It'll be no less than a catastrophe.

Raise your heart not your hand,
That is the only human way.
If you are forced to raise your hand,
Raise it only to shield, not to slay.

Hand raised to shield is human,
Hand raised to slay is animal.
Voice raised in justice is human,
Voice raised in hate is animal.

It is a cruel, cruel world,
Even for peace you gotta be a fighter.
Not all fighters are lovers,
But every true lover is a natural fighter.

The fight for love has nothing to do,
With guns and grenades.
To fight for love means,
To stand unarmed yet unbent.

In the face of an army of tyrants,
In the face of a pack of gun-bearing wolves,
Stand armed only by your backbone unbent,
To preserve life and liberty
for your loved ones, despite your wounds.

Either guns or love, you gotta make a choice.
Either bullets or beauty, you gotta choose.
Wage a war for love unarmed,
whenever danger looms.

Only a lover can put fairness in warfare,
Only a lover can take the world across wars.
This is no work for the puny lover of body,
Only a lover of heart can achieve such gargantuan task.

Freedom of religion can exist only,
Where there is religion of freedom.
Freedom of love can exist only,
Where there is love of freedom.

Freedom of choice can exist only,
Where there is choice of freedom.
Freedom of being can exist only,
Where there are beings of freedom.

Freedom is a tiny word that goes a long way,
It is a realm where there is no you and me.
My freedom is incomplete till another is free,
Till all of us are free, none of us are free.

Love is freedom, freedom is love,
One who knows love, knows freedom.
A lover also knows accountability,
Without which no freedom is freedom.

42

Part 8

There is not one but two freedom,
One is animal and the other is human.
By freedom one implies the human one,
Animal freedom is but reckless exploitation.

Lover's freedom is that of a human,
Which is indistinguishable from accountability.
Where there is love there is freedom,
Where there is freedom that must be responsibility.

Lovers often break the law,
Yet there can be no law without love.
The day when love and law combine,
That is the birth of a civilized epoch.

To love is to make law,
To hate is to break law.
To love is to cause order,
To hate is to be an outlaw.

So I say, love each and love all,
Till your heart begins to fail.
Love is the seed of all order,
Love is the kingdom beyond the veil.

To be wounded in love,
Is to be healed by love.
To be broken in love,
Is to awaken in love.

In love, brokenness is wholeness,
In love, suffering is serenity.
Better love and suffer all the way,
Than turn bitter and grumpy out of envy.

Ever since the self got unselfed,
What is envy I don't know.
I have never been out of love,
To envy another's glow.

To have and to hold,
Is the ideal condition.
But lover is the one,
Who loves even in destitution.

To have love and to know love,
Are not one and the same thing.
To have love is not a big deal,
To know love is the lover's rising.

Sana bir mektup yazmak lazım,
Fırsat bulursan biraz oku.
Ne kadar katlanacağım, bilmem ama,
Fırsat bulursan biraz oku.

Diyorlar ki, zaman her şeyi iyileştirir,
Ama benim durumuma hiç ilaç yok.
Fırsat bulursan gel, elimi tut biraz,
Sen yanımdaysan, ölüm bile ölüm yok.

Dünya bana kahraman diyor, bilge adam diyor,
Ama bu kahramanın kalbi kıyamette yaşıyor.
Dünyanın zehrini tekrar ve tekrar içerek,
Bu aşksız fakirin ruhu çok ama çok acıyor.

Okuyacaksın, yoksa fırlatacaksın,
bilmiyorum.
Ama can olduğu sürece,
seni çok ama çok bekliyorum.

Zaman hiçbir şey konuşmaz,
ama gözyaşları çok konuşuyor.
Gözyaşlarını görerek bile,
kalpsiz dünya sessizce duruyor.

Part 9

Gotta write a letter to you,
If you get a chance, do read it.
Don't know how long I can endure,
But if you get a chance, do read it.

They say, time heals all wounds,
But there is no treatment to my condition.
If you get a chance, come and sit by me,
With you by my side even death is salvation.

The world hails one a pillar, an epitome of strength,
But inside, one battles with apocalypse everyday.
Sipping poison like delicate wine, time after time,
A loveless fakir gets used to be used and thrown away.

Read me or rip me,
it is up to you.
So long as the heart beats,
I'm waiting for you.

Waiting usually causes exhaustion,
Yet the anticipation of love is sheer joy.
Though such joy isn't without tears,
Only a lover can wait without a devious ploy.

Time tells nothing, only tears do,
Time heals nothing, only tears do.
Yet amidst all the tears shed in love,
A heartless world stands silent as statue.

The world has made a tradition out of statuedom,
Anybody who defies it is deemed as nutcase.
Statuedom is stardom, according to the world,
To live otherwise is to be labeled a mental case.

It is a shallow, shallow world,
That says one way and lives another.
They buy most books based on jacket, yet,
They yell, don't judge a book by its cover.

If you must measure a person,
Measure by their passion, not passport.
If you must measure a person,
Measure by their wounds, not wallet.

Wallets wither, passports expire,
But a character of light keeps shining.
You can dollarize a land, but not a heart,
To put a pricetag on a person is dehumanizing.

It's okay to dollarize economy,
What's not okay is to dollarize humanity.
It's okay to monetize skills,
What's not okay is to monetize integrity.

The purpose of money is,
To keep mind and body together.
Not to separate the mind,
From society, from collective welfare.

Welfare of one is the welfare of all,
Welfare of all is the welfare of one.
Where there is love there is welfare,
In the absence of love everything is wrong.

Love shows the way, for love is the way,
Lack of way is actually lack of love.
Heart shows the way, for heart is the way,
Head under heart, thus walks the human dove.

Human needs no gun, for human is the gun.
Human needs no rose, for human is the rose.
Human needs no rosary, for human is the rosary,
Every human is bulldozer, with a single lovedose.

54

Part 10

56

Sen iste,
Bin defa din değiştireceğim.
Sen iste,
Bütün atalarımı bırakacağım.

Sen iste,
Bin defa milliyet değiştireceğim.
Sen sadece emret, canım benim,
Senin her arzunla yeni bir hayat yazacağım.

If it is the will of love,
I'll convert a thousand religions.
If it is the will of love,
I'll disown a thousand ancestors.

If it is the will of love,
I'll change a thousand nationalities.
You just command, my sweet,
Love's wish is life's theology.

All can be compromised for love,
But love must be compromised for nothing.
Sacrifice all identity at the altar of life,
Life will show you the identity with meaning.

What is our identity!
Who the hell are we really!
Who the hell cares, for it's time,
To choose love over identity.

Only life is important,
Only love is real.
All else is fantasy,
All else is trivial.

Love never asks you to erase your past,
Love never attempts to erase your identity.
Love accepts your past and expands your present,
Love embraces you as you, and empowers your identity.

Identity is meant to serve life,
Life is not the servant of identity.
Identity is meant to serve love,
Love is not the servant of identity.

Ancestry is meant to serve the human,
Human is not the servant of ancestry.
Enemies of love are enemies of life,
Enemies of love are enemies of humanity.

Culture can either further the cause of life,
Or it can hinder life, love and liberty.
If it hinders, it belongs in the dump,
If it furthers, it is an ally of humanity.

Our ancestors are not
the vanguards of our life, we are.
What they deemed as right and wrong,
Has got nothing to do with who we are.

We are much more than a mouthpiece for a culture,
We are much more than a showpiece of our ancestry.
I am not saying that we gotta cut off our roots,
But we mustn't let roots become chains of slavery.

To give chains the reins of life,
Is sheer desecration of life.
Amidst a world full of dead desecrators,
Stand alone if needed but stand alive.

It is far better to walk alone in love,
Than to walk with a pack of hatehogs.
Ten days of life in love is far better,
Than a 100 years of slaving as watchdog.

Part 11

62

Life begins at the edge of your identity,
One that is imposed by environment.
To be born out of a person is animal,
To grow out of divisionism is sapiens.

If the bible comes and peddles phobia,
I'll burn such bible to ashes.
If the koran comes and peddles violence,
I'll tear up such koran to pieces.

If the vedas come and peddle superstition,
I'll crush such filth to pulp with my foot.
If the constitution comes and peddles war,
As concerned parent I'll grab their makers,
And spank out all their dormant good.

Even if some two-bit God comes,
And peddles division,
I'll divide him so many times,
Even to his apostles,
He'll bear no recognition.

Love is my religion,
The one I love is my deity.
Anyone who impedes my worship,
Will forget what is gaiety.

And a little word of advise to those,
Priming their guns, swords and tridents.
When a volcano erupts,
Insects are supposed to run,
Not hide behind bows, arrows and bibles.

I am the spirit that is and has been,
I am the father, I am the son.
In tragedy I am volcano,
In triumph I am vicdan (conscience).

Do yourself a favor,
Trade in your bows and arrows
for some common sense.
You have seen a lover's love,
I beg you, please don't invite
a lover's wrath, my friend.

I am not your run-of-the-mill
defenseless scholar.
I am a shield to the humans,
But to animals - a disaster.

Brain is mightier than bullets,
Heart is mightier than the homunculus.
When a 3 pound brain falls on bigoted bugs,
There is no running, only burning to cinders.

But if I choose to have mercy on you,
And allow you to take my life.
Rest assured of one thing, my friend,
Even my corpse will radiate love and light.

If lovers are to disappear
from the face of the earth,
So will earth from the Milky Way.
If the heart is to disappear
from the human psyche,
So will all the human way.

All roads lead to love, if not,
Such roads have no purpose.
Let love lead all your roads,
Because once this life is gone,
There is no second chance.

Put this life to some good use,
Live this life as a living human.
Only living human is the one who loves,
Rest are just walking dead disguised as human.

Don't hide, my love,
Let the light shine from within.
Once the heart is let to shine,
All that is right will come running.

Part 12

To see love we gotta be love,
To walk the path is to make the path.
To be the hand is to have the hand,
To lose the heart is to have the heart.

If the head disappears from earth,
There'll be no progress whatsoever.
But if the heart disappears from earth,
There'll be no human whatsoever.

Head is a part of human,
But it is not the whole of human.
The heart on the other hand,
Is just another name for the human.

There's a difference between
what we need to have and what we need to be.
Head is what we need to have,
Heart is what we need to be.

Honorable, Energetic, Amiable,
Revolutionary, Transformer,
That is the definition of HEART.
Whereas the HEAD is sometimes
Heart's Eccentric Ally,
sometimes just Doofus, nothing much.

Every lover is doofus,
Every lover is genius.
Genius of head is cool,
Genius of heart is precious.

With enough labor anybody
can be genius of the head.
But if there is no love,
No labor can make a lover,
even out of one with a hundred heads.

Headless heart is vulnerable,
But heartless head is unbearable.
We need both with heart in charge,
It's the heart that knows,
what is actually sensible.

In a society of civilized humans,
Heart comes first, head second,
And belief comes last.
In a society of civilized humans,
Love comes first, culture second,
And ideology comes last.

Love is service,
Love is rule.
To serve is to love,
To serve is to rule.

None rules the world except the servant,
None pleasures the world except the lover.
There is no living but dying for love,
There's no other way but to love beyond desire.

Love is not a desire,
Love is determination.
Love is not a sentiment,
Love is annihilation.

Be annihilated, be insulted,
Be stripped of all your reputation.
Lover's reputation is in unreputation,
Human's honor is in loving annihilation.

Let love be the highest opinion,
Let love be the supreme belief.
Without love all growth is decay,
Without love don't even breathe.

One breath taken in love is worth more,
Than a thousand years of cold existence.
Breathe love, drink love, live love,
Keep breaking yourself in love,
till you wake up to whole magnificence.

Part 13

74

There is no wholeness,
Where there is no brokenness.
To be broken in pieces for love,
Is to find wholeness.

Forget who you are, forget what you are,
Forget all you are taught about identity.
A dehydrated world is least qualified,
To preach lessons on hydration of humanity.

Inhumans are but examples,
of how a human must never be.
Learn from their missteps surely,
But never pledge them your loyalty.

Lover's loyalty is to love alone,
All else is to take a backseat.
Even if Lord Almighty demands obedience,
Love comes first to a lover, then Lords and Ladies.

In love there is no loyalty,
You pledge loyalty to kings, queens and stateheads.
The valley of love is beyond such petty notions
of loyalty and obedience.

All lovers are servant anyway,
It's not about loyalty, but life.
All lovers are kings and queens,
It's not about authority, but light.

Where there is authority, there can't be love,
Where there is control, there can't be life.
To control love is to castrate love,
To have authority is to lose all light.

So burn, my friend,
Burn for the pleasure of burning.
Birds don't care about control,
Their very nature is singing.

Burn like the sun, my friend,
Innocent yet magnificent!
Without the sun there is no life,
Yet you never hear it talk about reimbursement.

Love with an agenda,
Is no love but a transaction.
Either love or don't,
There is no compensation.

Make the other smile without agenda,
That is a lover's compensation.
Make the other's tear disappear,
That is a lover's true satisfaction.

But if you are still thinking,
In terms of 'empath not doormat',
Then love is not your métier.
You better open a liquor shop,
At least a lot of dough will come your way.

If we can't be a doormat to the people we love,
We don't deserve to have them.
Choose one with heart over all else,
And you won't have to regret meeting them.

We regret because we love with eyes,
One who loves with heart has no regrets.
Everybody regrets, their beloved doesn't listen,
Why - because we never cross our selfish fence.

We've been fencing behind fences for ages,
Millennia went by yet we are still savages.
To make things worse instead of growing up,
We keep obsessing over make-belief problems.

Part 14

Never say, 'I am a sinner,
I only need to pray, there is no need for deeds'.
Always say, I am the love,
I am the lift that the world needs.

Lesser the needs,
Deeper the deeds.
Deeper the deeds,
Lesser the needs.

When greed gets no heed,
Heart and head cause the deed.
When greed of matter overwhelms the being,
all they talk is mindless creed.

Nothing happens for a reason,
But a human determined can turn the table.
The question is, will you make something happen,
Or keep on believing myths as spinally disabled.

With all our understanding of the speed of light,
We're yet to cross the distance from heart to heart.
With all our fancy equipment of communication,
We are yet to listen to those unheard.

To hear is to be heard,
To see is to be seen.
To speak for is to be spoken for,
Clean mind makes the world clean.

Just mind makes the world just,
Just heart makes the head just.
Just civilians make democracy just,
Just household makes the neighborhood just.

The world inside is the world outside,
When there is love inside there is love outside.
The beauty inside is the beauty outside,
When there is sense inside there is sense outside.

To sense nonsense is the highest sense,
To sense love is even higher sense.
To put all sense under love is higher still,
If there's no love in senses, all sense is nonsense.

Love sensible is no love,
You can have either sensibility or love.
If love doesn't wipe out all our fake order,
It ain't love but mere ravings of the daft.

Love alone brings order eternal,
Order brought by law is shortlived.
Only selfless lovers make good lawmakers,
All others are just playing make belief.

Let love come as apocalypse and wipe out,
All that is rigid, all that is prehistoric.
Welcome love into your life as a purifying force,
Let it bring you to life anew and terrific.

Life is terrific when life has love but,
To have love and to have lover ain't the same.
Lover isn't one who has someone to love them back,
But one who radiates love,
despite living in drought without rain.

None knows the value of rain,
But the land of eternal drought.
None knows the value of love,
But the heart that loves despite hurt.

Only the one who knows pain,
Can love another without gain.
Only the heart that knows hurt,
Can help another without rain.

Part 15

Bir damla yağmur için,
Bu kalp uzun zamandır bekliyor.
Bulutlar geldi, bulutlar gitti,
Parçalanan ruh daha da paramparça oluyor.

Paramparça olmak nasıl bir duygu,
Çok iyi biliyorum ben.
Bu yüzden, her derdimi,
Mutlu bir gülümsemeyle sakladım.

For a single drop of hearty rain,
I've been waiting for so long.
Clouds come and clouds go but,
The moment an image turns human,
all possibility of rain is gone.

The more a being is broken in love,
The more whole a being becomes.
Awareness is born of brokenness,
It's in darkness that insight comes.

Karanlıkta bu kalp çok parlar,
Karanlık bize yolu gösterir.
Kalbini kaybetme be deli insan,
Seviyorum söylemek çok kolay,
Ama karanlıkta sevmek, sadece,
Gerçek bir aşık için mümkündür.

It is in darkness that,
heart shines the brightest,
It is darkness that shows the lane.
Don't lose heart, o lover loco,
Everybody can love when happy,
Only a few can love in pain.

Broken beings are living beings,
One who isn't broken isn't alive.
To walk in the light is quite easy,
To walk in the dark is the walk of light.

No sabes desamor, no sabes amor,
Corazón roto es corazón vivo.
Incluso cadáveres pueden caminar en la luz,
En la oscuridad solo pueden caminar los vivos.

Vamos, seamos pioneros de la luz,
Bebamos todo el veneno del dolor!
Beber veneno y ofrecer un sueño,
Es la primera naturaleza del amador.

Come, let us be pioneers of light,
Let us feast on the world's darkness!
To drink poison and deliver elixir,
Is the first nature of a sapiens.

Every sapiens is atom bomb,
Every sapiens is a power plant.
Reckless mind is mayhem machine,
Hateless mind is lightland.

Land of love is godland,
There's nothing else more divine.
Divinity is but a lesser synonym,
There's no god, only lover divine.

Aşk vatanımdır,
Milliyetim aşık.
Benim adım insan,
İnancım insanlık.

Faith is subordinate to love,
Philosophy is subordinate to love,
Science is subordinate to love.
Until you feel it in your bones,
You've got plenty dust to wash off.

La fe está subordinada al amor,
La filosofía está subordinada al amor.
La ciencia está subordinada al amor,
Sentir esto en tu alma es ser humano.

90

Part 16

Tu mano en mi mano,
Nos haremos humano.
Tu corazón con mi corazón,
Encontraremos la salvación.

All stories of salvation are myth,
True salvation is when two become one.
Let the I go, let the You go,
Then you shall taste tangible salvation.

Senin olduğun her yer cennet bana,
Sensiz cennet bile cehennemdir,
Canım sana ihtiyacım var, anlamıyorsun!
Dinimden vazgeçtim, milletimle mücadele ettim,
Ben daha ne yapayım söyle, ben dinliyorum!

There is no heaven without the human,
All nature is hell without sentiment.
Long enough nature has kept us animals,
It's time to move out of her basement.

Aşkın olduğu her yer cennet,
Aşksız cennet bile cehennemdir.
Bir anlık aşk için yüz yıllık şöhreti,
Feda etmek, benim için çok kolaydir.

Heartshot over headshot,
Heartbeat over pursebeat.
That's how we move forward,
That's how we cause uplift.

We are our own cause,
We are our own effect.
When that cause is full of love,
Nothing can stop it from coming to effect.

The being is the bridge,
The being is the wall.
Be a being and you are bridge,
Be a thing and you are wall.

Un puente de amor es más
valiente que cien muros de apatía.
Un puente de paz es más
valiente que cien fronteras de guerra.

Than a hundred walls of hate,
One bridge of love is mightier.
One bridge of peace is braver,
Than a hundred borders of war.

Aşkın bir köprüsü,
nefretin bin duvarından
daha cesurdur.
Barışın bir köprüsü,
savaşın bin sınırlardan
daha cesurdur.

One illiterate lover does more for the world,
than a hundred lawyers.
One illiterate peacemaker does more for the world,
than a hundred policymakers.

Policy is to be guided by peace not purse,
World is to be run by love not wallet.
Money can buy life's sustenance not life itself,
Let love be the judge and,
the world will have all the sustenance.

Ben sadece basit bir insanım.
Ben ne bileyim jeopolitik meselesi!
Ama her aşık kendine yeni bir dünyadır,
Bu dünyada aşk kanundur, ve siyaset tarihtir.

I am just an ordinary human,
What do I know about fancy matters of geopolitics!
But every lover is progress incarnate,
In that world love is law and politics obsolete.

96

Part 17

Until partisanism is history,
There is no tomorrow.
Until love is the supreme choice,
Inhumanity is not gonna go.

Hasta que el partidismo sea historia,
no hay mañana.
Hasta que amor sea la elección suprema,
No hay esperanza para la humanidad.

Choose to love, choose to live,
Choose to transcend all belief.
Be the being to choose the beings,
Over, above and beyond habit.

When hate is habit,
It's the hate that we gotta 86.
Our ancestors taught us cultural 69,
It's time we outgrow such nonsense archaic.

When integration is deemed illegal,
Every civilian must become an outlaw.
When human rights violation becomes law,
Everyday the civilians must break the law.

Love is answerable to no law,
Light is answerable to no darkness.
When traditions make a question mark out of life,
Each lover must rise as the answer of conscience.

Vicdanlı ol, be deli aşık!
Sen vicdanını kaybedersen
dünyadan tüm vicdan kaybolacak!
Senin vicdanın dünyanın vicdanıdır,
Senin aşkın yolu ilerlemenin yolu olacak.

Be conscientious, oh brave lover!
If you fail in conscience, so will the world.
Your conscience is seed for the world's conscience,
Every step you take in love is the world's step forward.

Forward ever, backward never!
Accepting always, assuming never!
Upward always, downward never!
Transformer always, troll never!

Inclusive always, divisive never!
Lover always, labeler never!
Caring always, doubting never!
Empowering always, discouraging never!

Kâinatin tek hakikat, aşktır,
Aşktan başka her şey yalan.
Kalbin kıyameti, nefrettir,
Nefretten vazgeçen her biri, mucize insan.

Only truth in the cosmos is love,
Save love, all else is a lie.
Rise of hate is the apocalypse of heart,
Heart run by hate is a heart gone awry.

Wake up from hate,
Walk up to love.
Without basic decency,
All life is junk.

It's a junkyard outside,
Because it's a junkyard inside.
Junk is junk, even if it's tradition,
So you gotta make a choice - junk or life.

Expansion is a requirement of life,
Exclusion is antithesis of a world civilized.
Expansion pushes evolution forward,
Whereas exclusion dumps us all the way behind.

Part 18

104

You don't eliminate hate against a culture,
By yelling about the hate against that culture.
You eliminate hate against a culture,
By being the very cream of that culture.

It is not about being
an example of perfection.
It's just about giving up,
All hateful reciprocation.

We don't eliminate hate,
By turning hater ourselves.
We eliminate hate by being
the uplift ourselves.

Integration is just a fancy term,
the presence of which
indicates our backwardness.
In a society of practicing humans,
integration is not a philosophy,
but an everyday common sense.

Why does humanity have to be a philosophy!
Why does love have to be an ideology!
Those who don't fathom love beyond the books,
Won't get it with even a million philosophies.

Lovers don't have philosophy,
Lovers don't have ideology.
Love is too grand to be contained,
By the puny domain of philosophy.

Love is too grand to be explained by chemistry,
If it could, chemists would be the greatest lovers.
To analyze love is to paralyze love,
To do politics on peace is to facilitate war.

They call it diplomacy,
I call it dick-lo-messy.
When your beloved is sick,
With the disease,
Do you do diplomacy!

It is all about the illusive separation,
between personal and social.
Phony humans have one parameter for personal life,
And completely another for the one social.

There is no personal,
There is no social.
It's all either love's reflection,
Or nothing at all.

There is no society, only family.
There is no responsibility, only love.
There is no death, only immortality.
But to fathom these you gotta be in love.

It's not romantic love,
It's not platonic love.
It's not sexual love,
It's not intellectual love.

A constipated world concocted
these constipated terms.
You for one, love beyond facts,
figures and traditions.

Make love your tradition,
And all light will follow.
Make the heart your guide,
And all reason will follow.

Reason used against love is treason,
Such reason is but sheer descent.
Intellect used to belittle love,
Is not intellect but derangement.

Part 19

If reason makes you feel entitled,
Such reason is worse than ignorance.
If reason makes you responsible,
Only then it has a purposeful radiance.

Purpose of reason is to empower love,
Not to be an obstruction of jackassery.
If intellect doesn't make the human humble,
It is worth not even a counterfeit penny.

Grab a flower,
Tell me what it's worth!
If you can, you don't know love.
If you can't, there is hope for love.

A tiny flower is more precious,
than a million nuclear weapons.
One smile on the lips of the beloved,
produces more gigawatts
than a hundred power plants.

Power comes from love,
Power comes from attachment.
Those who say attachment is weakness,
Have no idea of life's true wholeness.

There is no ascension without attachment,
Fear of attachment is but fear of life.
For once in your life, let go of all fears,
Submit yourself whole at the mercy of light.

In love there is no success, there's no failure,
Those who think otherwise are slaves of reward.
If you love another like you love your cellphone,
You are better off without the labor of love.

A transactional mind is but an insult of love.
Either love or don't, there is no half-loving.
Measure not the light of love by the laws of red light.
At least the red light doesn't pretend purity,
Unlike the civil society with their half-loving.

Love whole and lose everything,
Discover yourself anew in love's martyrdom.
Without reservation let love reshape you
down to your very last atom.

Love with your every atom,
No rigidity must stand in the way.
Only those deserve love who prefer love,
Over and above all the historical ways.

History isn't made by the smart or rigid,
History is made by the lovers alone.
History made by smartness alone,
Is no more than caves of silicon.

Anybody with half a brain,
Can make history, that's not a big deal.
It's more important to make a humane history,
than just history - that's the human deal.

Lovers and haters both can make history.
Are you willing to live the one made by haters!
It's the lovers that make history human,
Whereas the haters only cause disasters.

Her insan bir mucizedir,
Her insan misafirdir.
İnsanın tatlı bir merhabası,
cennetten davettir.

Every lover is a miracle,
Every lover is a traveler.
One smile of a lover is equivalent,
of a hundred poems - hence, a transformer.

Part 20

Eğer seviyorsa çocuk gibi sev,
kuru soğuk gibi değil.
Eğer seviyorsa, gönlünle sev,
gözlerinle değil.

Life is too short
to be wasted as a loveless trap.
Life spent in love,
Is a life well deserved.

Sevgili ol, sevgili kal!
Bu hayatta sevgiden daha
hiçbir şey önemli değil.
Barış gelecek, barış kalacak,
Ama önce insan insan olmalı, hayvan değil.

Be a lover, stay a lover!
Love is the other name of life.
Peace will come, peace will stay!
But first humans have to rise above animal life.

Peace across prejudice,
Harmony across hatred, that is sapiens.
To conquer prejudice is to make peace,
All it takes is to outgrow the old ways.

Be brave enough to belittle your belief,
Before you belittle a person.
Be human enough to belittle yourself,
Before you indulge in condescension.

Lovers don't fathom
superior, inferior.
They're driven only
by a sacrificial desire.

I see no high,
I see no low.
All I see is potential,
kept trapped by bigoted row.

How immersed are you in peace,
That is the question.
How soaked are you in love,
That is the question.

There is no genius,
There is only involvement.
How much involved,
are you in your purpose,
That is the question.

Every lover is a genius,
But not every genius is in love.
Genius without love is genius misguided,
for genius without heart,
causes nothing but havoc.

You know what genius means,
It means Gentle I in Us.
But who the hell cares about genius!
The touch of love makes
genius even out of a doofus.

I am a doofus,
I've been a doofus all my life.
Only the doofus gets to live life,
while the intellectuals
waste it on worthless strife.

Love makes you humble,
Love makes you accepting.
Love strengthens the backbone,
And makes a lover uncompromising.

There can be compromise on identity,
There can compromise on ideology.
But there is no compromise on love,
There is no compromise on humanity.

Part 21

What right do you have
to call yourself human,
When your very life is founded
on the compromise of humanity!
What right do you have to love and laughter,
When your life is a burial ground
of love, laughter and luminosity!

When lunacy is the norm,
Luminosity is deemed sickness.
When division is the way of life,
Peace, love and harmony are inconvenience.

We gotta rise above the inconvenience,
We gotta rise above ourselves.
When the wellbeing of love
is the wellbeing of ours,
That's when we manifest our luminescence.

There is light, I say,
There is lift, I say.
For once seek it not here and there,
Instead give your life away.

Life is amplified when you give it away,
Heart is humanized When you burn it to cinders.
Understanding rises when assumption ends,
Realization begins when argumentation withers.

Will the light, and there is light,
Unwill the hate, and there is love.
Will the lift, and there is uplift,
Unwill the prejudice, and lo flies the dove!

Lovers are duffers
who make the world worth living in.
Erase all the lovers, let's see,
how long you persist with
all your unreal engine!

Erase the insanity of love,
And you erase all possibility of sanity.
Erase the madness of lover's sacrifice,
You only facilitate a society of animality.

It's okay for the animals to be animal,
But it's a tragedy for a human
to be anything but a lover.
It's okay for google to answer
without feeling, but a human ought to
have feeling in their every answer.

Love is the ultimate answer,
Rest are just wingmen.
Intellect is doormat to love,
Tradition is doormat to love,
thus lives the lover sentient.

Kusura bakma, canım benim,
Benim için Allah'tan
daha önemli sensin.
Kusura bakma, güzel gözlerim,
Benim için en büyük ibadet sensin.

All the lords turn dust,
In front of one ounce of love.
All worship turn bleak,
In front of a hopeless hug.

Yanında kal ya da uzak dur,
Hayatım artık sana emanet son nefese kadar.
İnsan yanımda kalan birini değil,
Kalbinde kalan birini sever.

Stay near me, or walk away from me,
Now this life is but love's vessel.
Near, afar, love knows no distance,
Out of sight out of mind, is but law of the animal.

Love that hasn't yet conquered
the concept of distance,
Isn't love but a mockery of love.
Mind that hasn't yet learnt
to rise above the concept of body,
Isn't mind but a bag of dirt.

Part 22

Biz neyiz? Aşk askeri.
Biz ne yüzden kâinatta doğduk?
Birbirinize destek olmak yüzden.
Biz neyiz? Aşk ateşi.
Biz ne yüzden kâinatta doğduk?
Birbirimizin derdine ilaç olmak yüzden.

What are we? Soldiers of love.
Why did we come to existence?
To be each other's ladder in life.
What are we? Boulders of love.
Why did we come to existence?
To bulldozer each other's crisis in life.

Eğer seviyorsa,
gözlerinle değil, gönlünle sev.
Eğer yaşıyorsa,
nefesinle değil, niyetinle yaşa.

Kaldırmak istiyorsa,
Kalbini kaldır, elini değil.
Kazanmak istiyorsa,
Dualar kazan, paralar değil.

Love not with mere bod, but heart,
Live without paranoia, beyond the band.
If you must raise something at all,
Raise your heart, not hand.

Aşk tehlikedeyken,
Her aşık kanundur,
Her aşık adalettir.
Aşk tehlikedeyken,
Her aşık kıyamettir.

When love is in danger,
Every lover is law,
Every lover is justice.
When love is in danger,
Every lover is apocalypse.

Si el amor está en peligro,
Todo amante es ley,
Todo amante es justicia.
Si el amor está en peligro,
Todo amante es chupacabra.

If everybody fell in love, really, truly, genuinely,
There'll be no government left,
and no trace of political ideology.

If everybody fell in love, really, truly, genuinely,
There'll be no church left,
and no trace of biblical foolery.

Even an animal can love the body,
It takes a human to love the person.
Even an animal can love with genital,
It takes a human to love across arousal.

To be horny and to be in love,
Are two different things.
When horny you want release,
When in love you don't wanna be released.

Yes, it is true that I want you,
But I want you at your
own free will and natural pace.
For that if I have to wait an eternity,
I shall do so without regret.

There is no reality,
Only hallucination.
A lover's reality is self-sacrifice,
A snob's reality is self-preservation.

Ben askerim, aşk askeriyim!
Beni öldürmek çok kolay ama,
Kalbimin aşkını nasıl öldüreceksin!
Adim Naskar, herkes deli Naskar diyor,
Beni vurmak çok kolay ama,
Bu deliliğe nasıl vuracaksın!

Part 23

Donde no hay locura
de amor en la vida,
No hay sensibilidad,
No hay vida.

Deli insan doğru insan,
Deliliksiz insan insan yok.
İnsan insanlık için deli değilse,
Böyle bir hayat insan hayatı yok.

Bonkers human is righteous human,
All others are sleeping mice.
If you ain't bonkers for love and life,
There is no love, there is no life.

There is no progress without madness,
There is no growth without madness.
But there's a difference
between madness and primitiveness.

In a world of sane half-lovers,
Sanity is primitiveness.
In a world of sane never-livers,
Sanity is lifelessness.

Love bears all and bares all,
With no reserve and no preserve.
Destiny is master to the shallow,
But servant to the braveheart lovers.

In love's domain bravery is child's play,
Yet it seems a big deal to those on the outside.
In love's domain sacrifice is first nature,
Yet it seems absurd to those without lovesight.

There is no greater sight than that of love,
Love brings might, height, light and much more.
For once in your life just fall without agenda,
And you shall attain flight like never before.

To fly, first you gotta fall.
To rise, first you gotta fall.
To shine, first you gotta fall.
To be the light you are,
there's no other way but to fall.

So fall, my friend, fall in love!
Fall, without agenda, across fear.
Keep your fear, but let it not tear you,
If you must be torn apart,
only love has the right to tear.

Let love tear you apart,
Through the cracks come luminosity.
Let love wipe out all that you are,
So that you may find out
what you are meant to be.

Meant to be or not be,
All of it is made of mind.
Once the lover makes their mind,
Nature herself conspires
in your favor day and night.

Just once in your life
gut up to walk at night.
And light will come chasing
from every direction,
regardless of foresight.

Foresight has little significance,
If it isn't driven by love.
Let love come and possess you like crazy,
And all creeds will be cut to half.

Civilization comes from the eyes of the lover,
If a lover doesn't see it, it won't come to light.
A lover doesn't need to be taught civic duty,
For a lover needs no law to tell what is right.

Part 24

What is right, what is wrong?
To question with intellect, that's wrong.
Ask a being of love what is right,
they won't know, but observe their action,
you'll find out what you're doing wrong.

You don't ask what is right,
what is wrong,
you just fall in love and find out.
The most important questions in life
are not meant to be asked,
But to be lived and felt aloud.

Feel the question and you'll feel the answer.
Feel the love and you'll feel the light.
Be no slave like others to some puny intellect,
Feel the love first, then you'll know,
how much and when intellect is right.

Lover knows best,
but not the one who loves with eyes.
Lover knows best, I say again,
one who loves with heartsight.

Where there is heart,
there is sight.
Where there is assumption,
there is only night.

Night doesn't disappear when the head wakes up,
Night disappears when the heart wakes up.
Storms don't disappear
when the wind stops blowing,
Storms fade when you befriend them,
and walk with your eyes up.

Day and night are mental constructs,
Chemicals cause daybreak,
Chemicals cause nightfall.
For a being lost in love,
what is day, what is night!
In front of love, all duality is trivial.

It ain't about balancing duality,
It's about losing all sense of duality.
Dualities thrive on self-obsession,
Transcend the self and lo comes serendipity.

All talk about all sorts of nonsense,
about magic and miracle.
Yet they remain oblivious to the fact,
that love is nature's greatest miracle.

Love is nature's greatest miracle,
A lover is the only miracle-worker.
While cavemen obsess over stories of miracle,
A lover's single smile acts as transformer.

There is no transformation without annihilation,
And no annihilation is possible without love.
Annihilation of the self
is resurrection of the being in love.

Birth is not birth, for many die old
without ever being born.
To be born you gotta die to yourself,
otherwise, you are just walking unborn.

Unborn we are,
unborn must we stay!
Why not just give it all up,
throw all selfishness far away!

Selfishness is poison on the fabric of love,
Selfishness is poison on the fabric of society.
With so much at stake, only hope is
to embrace love's absurdity.

Absurdity delivers awakening,
Awakening of the human
from the animal body.
All animals eat, sleep, mate and die,
but very few realize humanity.

Part 25

146

Yes I am absurd, I am impossible,
Yet I've made that impossible my life.
Only a lover will know what it means,
Only with love you'll see my light.

To the selfish, I don't exist,
To the selfless, I never died.
To the hater, I am worthless,
To the lover, I cannot be priced.

There is no I, there is no you,
There is only possibility of love.
I am only a manifestation
of the universal spirit of love.

From afar you only see my light,
Come close and you'll see,
you are made of the same light.
While lovers of matter exude darkness,
Lovers of mind are natural spring of light.

Come, be lost in my light,
so that I may be lost in your light.
Will you be companion in my pathlessness,
So that together we may give each other sight!

I am your sight,
As much as you are my sight.
We think the destination is a place,
but actually it is the state
of being each other's light.

Togetherness is the destination,
Companion is the journey.
Assimilation is the destination,
Annihilation is the journey.

But then again,
there is no destination,
only journey.
Companion is destination,
companion is the journey.

Companion is gospel,
Companion is the church.
Companion is the root,
Companion is the branch.

One who finds life
in companion's smile,
will find it everywhere,
in the Hudson, in the Nile.

For a lover there is only one continent,
The continent of companion.
For a lover there is only one ocean,
The ocean of union.

Earth is but a fiction,
Only love is real.
All truth is but lie,
Only love is real.

Home is not where the heart is,
Home is where the heart is lost.
Till there is nothing left but love,
All roof, all ground, are of no worth.

Until love is the roof,
and love is the ground,
everything inbetween is nothing.
Until love is the alpha,
love is the omega,
all the alphabets mean nothing.

Love is the seed,
love is the shade,
Love is the tree.
Try analyzing that with intellect,
with your puny psychology.

150

Part 26

Role of psychology is
to empower life with understanding,
not to paralyze it with judgment.
Understanding comes when
you understand nothing and just accept.

In the domain of love,
Analysis is paralysis.
Love founded on trust,
Needs no psychoanalysis.

Love and analysis are
antithesis of each other.
You can either have analysis,
or be a lover.

Lover lost in love
is their own therapist.
It's only the half-lovers
who need psychoanalysis.

If you have no sense of self,
There is no question of analysis.
If there is no 'you' to begin with,
There is no question of analyzing it.

In the most difficult situations of life,
Two lovers are each other's therapist.
If it's not the case, it ain't love to begin with,
But merely love's lookalike most primitive.

Love is its own sickness,
Love is its own cure.
What right does a third party have,
to step their condescending foot
into love's sacred door!

There may come even cure for cancer one day,
But there is no cure for love's trouble.
A lover doesn't seek cure for love's trouble,
It's only make believers who want to be sensible.

Love without trouble,
is not love but make belief.
Heart without hurt,
is not heart but make belief.

Agony is ornament
for a lover's soul.
To love through the pain
is the lover's supreme role.

It is not a lover's job to make sense,
Lover's role is to humanize all senses.
Role of animal senses is to stay contained,
Role of human senses is to extend themselves.

To sense the sense is nonsense,
To sense nonsense is ultimate sense of all.
This is possible only when you are lost,
This is possible only when you are in love.

All five senses
are of no worth,
If you don't have
that one sense,
the sense of love.

Sense yourself till
you sense nothing but love.
Break yourself till each crack reflects
the infinity of the heart.

Each of us is an explorer of infinity,
Yet we are trapped in vain by insecurity.
Wake up to love and you'll see,
all cages are fiction,
cooked up by knee-deep sanity.

Part 27

158

One day all of us will end up
six feet under, do you want your grave
to stink of hate or smell of love!
I for one will die of love despite hate,
so that even when I'm gone,
I leave behind nothing but love.

I want you to remember me
as the being who was living
amidst tremendous hate,
Yet he didn't submit,
even for a single second.

It is easy to take pleasure
in fictitious love stories.
It's okay, but don't ignore the living,
for the sake of characters imaginary.

Even I wrote a fictional love story,
but no fiction can substitute the life I've lived.
A real failed love story is worth more,
than a hundred successful myths.

In love, there is no failure,
there is no success, only life.
There may be failed love stories,
But there is no failed lover,
except those who love with eyes.

To fall in love is to conquer life,
Once you fall there is no coming back.
Once a lover always a lover,
From a veteran you can turn civilian,
from designation lover there's no coming back.

Lovers are the greatest veterans,
They are the veterans of war against hate.
And like a fallen veteran,
when one lover falls,
a thousand will take their place.

The torch of love must never go out,
To keep it lit is our supreme duty.
Give me ten lovers to die for love,
I'll give you the torch
of eternal love, light and liberty.

Only lovers and soldiers are living,
Rest are just dehydrating.
We are the infinity waiting to unfold,
But first we gotta give up all conditioning.

Only the sane can be conditioned,
Only the afraid can be brainwashed.
A lover is far too gone to be conditioned,
for no brainwash has any hold
over one who is heartwashed.

BIBLIOGRAPHY

Archer M., (2000), Being Human: The Problem of Agency. Cambridge University Press.

Adolphs R (2003) Cognitive neuroscience of human social behaviour. Nature Rev Neurosci 4: 165–178.

Adolphs R, Tranel D, Damasio AR (2003) Dissociable neural systems for recognizing emotions. Brain Cogn 52: 61–69.

Andresen, Jensine, and Robert Forman, eds. Cognitive Models and Spiritual Maps. Bowling Green, Ohio: Imprint Academic, 2000.

Bernstein R.J., (1971), Praxis and Action: Contemporary Philosophies of Human Activity. Philadelphia: University of Pennsylvania Press.

Bernstein R.J., (1976), The Restructuring Social and Political Thought.

Bogen, J.E.(1995a), 'On the neurophysiology of consciousness: Part I. An overview', Consciousness and Cognition, 4.

Bogen, J.E. (1995b), 'On the neurophysiology of consciousness: Part II. Constraining the semantic problem', Consciousness and Cognition, 4.

Bremner, J. D., R. Soufer, et al. (2001). "Gender differences in cognitive and neural correlates of remembrance of emotional words." Psychopharmacol Bull 35 (3).

Brothers, L. (2002). The social brain: A project for integrating primate behavior and neurophysiology in a new domain. In J. T. Cacioppo et al. (Eds.), Foundations in neuroscience. Cambridge, MA: MIT Press.

Buss, D. D. (2003). Evolutionary Psychology: The New Science of Mind, 2nd ed. New York: Allyn & Bacon.

Buss, D. M. (1989). "Conflict between the sexes: Strategic interference and the evocation of anger and upset." J Pers Soc Psychol 56 (5).

Buss, D. M. (1995). "Psychological sex differences. Origins through sexual selection." Am Psychol 50 (3).

Buss, D. M., and D. P. Schmitt (1993). "Sexual strategies theory: An evolutionary perspective on human mating." Psychol Rev 100 (2).

Chomsky Noam, (2016) Who Rules the World?

Churchland, P.S. (1986), Neurophilosophy (Cambridge, MA: The MIT Press).

Churchland, P.S. & Ramachandran, V.S. (1993), 'Filling in: Why Dennett is wrong', in Dennett and His Critics:

Demystifying Mind, ed. B. Dahlbom (Oxford: Blackwell Scientific Press).

Churchland, P.S., Ramachandran, V.S. & Sejnowski, T.J. (1994), 'A critique of pure vision', in Large- scale Neuronal Theories of the Brain, ed. C. Koch & J.L. Davis (Cambridge, MA: The MIT Press).

Crick, F. (1994), The Astonishing Hypothesis: The Scientific Search for the Soul (New York: Simon and Schuster).

Crick, F. (1996), 'Visual perception: rivalry and consciousness', Nature, 379.

Crick, F. & Koch, C. (1992), 'The problem of consciousness', Scientific American, 267.

d'Aquili, Eugene. "Senses of Reality in Science and Religion." Zygon 17, no 4 (1982) d'Aquili, Eugene. "The Biopsychological Determinants of Religious Ritual Behavior." Zygon 10, no. 1 (1975)

d'Aquili, Eugene. "The Myth-Ritual Complex: A Biogenetic Structural Analysis." Zygon 18, no. 3 (1983)

d'Aquili, Eugene, and Andrew Newberg. The Mystical Mind: Probing the Biology of Religious Experience. Minneapolis: Fortress Press, 1999.

Damasio, A. (1994) Descartes' Error: Emotion, Reason and the Human Brain. New York, Putnams.

Damasio, A. (1999) The Feeling of What Happens: Body, Emotion and the Making of Consciousness. London, Heinemann.

Darwin, C. (1859) On the Origin of Species by Means of Natural Selection. London, Murray.

Darwin, C. (1871) The Descent of Man and Selection in Relation to Sex. London, John Murray.

Dawkins, R. (1976) The Selfish Gene. Oxford, Oxford University Press; a new edition, with additional material, was published in 1989.

Dewhurst, Kenneth, and A. W. Beard. "Sudden Religious Conversions in Temporal Lobe Epilepsy." British Journal of Psychiatry 117 (1970)

Dewhurst K, Beard AW. Sudden religious conversions in temporal lobe epilepsy. 1970 Epilepsy Behav 2003

Devinsky O, Lai G. Spirituality and religion in epilepsy. Epilepsy Behav 2008.

E. Horvitz, "One Hundred Year Study on Artificial Intelligence: Reflections and Framing," ed: Stanford University, 2014.

Eckhart Meister, Selected Writings

Farah, M.J. (1989), 'The neural basis of mental imagery', Trends in Neurosciences, 10.

Freud, S. "Selected papers on hysteria and other psychoneuroses" Journal of Nervous and Mental Disease 1909.

Freud, S. "The Origin and Development of Psychoanalysis", 1910

Freud, S. "Psychopathology of everyday life", 1914

Freud, S. "Beyond the Pleasure Principle", 1920

Frith, C.D. & Dolan, R.J. (1997), 'Abnormal beliefs: Delusions and memory', Paper presented at the May, 1997, Harvard Conference on Memory and Belief.

Gay, Volney, ed. Neuroscience and Religion. Plymouth, UK: Lexington Books, 2009.

Gazzaniga, M. S. (1985). The social brain. New York: Basic Books.

Gazzaniga, M.S. (1993), 'Brain mechanisms and conscious experience', Ciba Foundation Symposium, 174.

Geschwind N. "Behavioural changes in temporal lobe epilepsy". Psychol Med. 1979.

Gellhorn, E., Kiely, W.F. "Mystical states of consciousness: neurophysiological and clinical aspects." J Nerv Ment Dis. 1972;154:399-405.

Gilbert SL, Dobyns WB, Lahn BT (2005) Genetic links between brain development and brain evolution. Nat Rev Genet 6.

Gray JA. The Psychology of Fear and Stress. 2nd ed. New York, NY: Cambridge University Press; 1988.

Gloor, P. (1992), 'Amygdala and temporal lobe epilepsy', in The Amygdala: Neurobiological Aspects of Emotion, Memory and Mental

Dysfunction, ed J.P. Aggleton (New York: Wiley-Liss).

Gross CG, Rocha-Miranda CE, Bender DB (1972) Visual properties of neurons in the inferotemporal cortex of the macaque. J Neurophysiol 35: 96–111.

Guevara Che, The Motorcycle Diaries, 1992

Hardy, G. H. (1940). Ramanujan. Cambridge: Cambridge University Press.

Hall, Daniel, Keith Meador, and Harold Koenig. "Measuring Religiousness in Health Research: Review and Critique." Journal of Religion and Health 47, no. 2 (2008)

Harris, Sam, Jonas Kaplan, Ashley Curiel, Susan Bookheimer, Marco Iacoboni, and Mark Cohen. "The Neural Correlates of Religious and Nonreligious Belief." PLoS One 4, no. 10 (October 1, 2009)

Halgren, E. (1992), 'Emotional neurophysiology of the amygdala within the context of human cognition', in The Amygdala: Neurobiological Aspects of Emotion, Memory and Mental Dysfunction, ed J.P. Aggleton (New York: Wiley-Liss).

Halligan PW, Fink GR, Marshal JC, Vallar G. 2003. Spatial cognition: evidence from visual neglect. Trends Cogn Sci.

Handbook of Emotions, Edited by Michael Lewis, Jeannette M. Haviland-Jones, and Lisa Feldman Barrett, The Guilford Press; 3rd edition (2010).

Hameroff, S.R. and Penrose, R. (1996) Conscious events as orchestrated space-time selections. Journal of Consciousness Studies 3(1), 36-53; also reprinted in J. Shear (ed.) (1997) Explaining Consciousness-The Hard Problem. Cambridge, MA, MIT Press, 177-95.

Harding, D.E. (1961) On Having no Head: Zen and the Re-Discovery of the Obvious. London, Buddhist Society.

Hardy, A. (1979) The Spiritual Nature of Man: A Study of Contemporary Religious Experience. Oxford, Clarendon Press.

Harre, R. and Gillett, G. (1994) The Discursive Mind. Thousand Oaks, CA, Sage.

Haugeland, J. (ed.) (1997) Mind Design II: Philosophy, Psychology, Artificial Intelligence. Cambridge, MA, MIT Press.

Hauser, M.D. (2000) Wild Minds: What Animals Really Think. New York, Henry Holt and Co.; London, Penguin.

Hilgard, E.R. (1986) Divided Consciousness: Multiple Controls in Human Thought and Action. New York, Wiley.

Hilton, E.N., Lundberg, T.R. Transgender Women in the Female Category of Sport: Perspectives on Testosterone Suppression and Performance Advantage. Sports Med 51, 199–214 (2021).

Hitler, Adolf. Mein Kampf, 1925

Hodgson, R. (1891) A case of double consciousness. Proceedings of the Society for Psychical Research 7, 221-58.

Hofstadter, D.R. and Dennett, D.C. (eds) (1981) The Mind's I: Fantasies and Reflections on Self and Soul. London, Penguin.

Holland, J. (ed.) (2001) Ecstasy: The Complete Guide: A Comprehensive Look at the Risks and Benefits of MDMA. Rochester, VT, Park Street Press.

Holmes, D.S. (1987) The influence of meditation versus rest on physiological arousal. In M. West (ed.)

The Psychology of Meditation. Oxford, Clarendon Press, 81-103.

Holmstrom, David. 1992, Christian Science Monitor

Holloway RL (1996) Evolution of the human brain. In: Lock A, Peters CR (eds) Handbook of human symbolic evolution. Oxford University Press, Oxford

Jeannerod M (1988) The neural and behavioural organization of goal-directed movements. Clarendon Press, Oxford.

Johnson-Frey SH, Maloof FR, Newman-Norlund R, Farrer C, Inati S, Grafton ST (2003) Actions or hand-objects interactions? Human inferior frontal cortex and action observation. Neuron 39: 1053–1058.

Jackson, F. (1982) Epiphenomenal qualia. Philosophical Quarterly 32, 127-36.

James, W. (1890) The Principles of Psychology (2 volumes). London, Macmillan.

James, W. (1902) The Varieties of Religious Experience: A Study in Human Nature. New York and London, Longmans, Green and Co.

Jansen, K. (2001) Ketamine: Dreams and Realities. Sarasota, FL, Multidisciplinary Association for Psychedelic Studies.

Jay, M. (ed.) (1999) Artificial Paradises: A Drugs Reader. London, Penguin.

Jaynes, J. (1976) The Origin of Consciousness in the Breakdown of the Bicameral Mind. New York, Houghton Mifflin.

Kandel, E. R. In Search of Memory: The Emergence of a New Science of Mind, W. W. Norton & Company (2007).

Kandel E. R. Schwartz JH, Jessel TM. Principles of neural sciences. New York; McGraw Hill, 2000.

Kanwisher, N. (2001) Neural events and perceptual awareness. Cognition 79, 89-113; also reprinted inS. Dehaene (ed.) The Cognitive Neuroscience of Consciousness. Cambridge, MA, MIT Press, 89-113.

Kihlström, J.F. (1996) Perception without awareness of what is perceived, learning without awareness of what is learned. In M. Velmans (ed.) The Science of Consciousness. London, Routledge, 23-46.

Kosslyn, S.M. (1980) Image and Mind. Cambridge, MA, Harvard University Press.

Kosslyn, S.M. (1988) Aspects of a cognitive neuroscience of mental imagery. Science 240, 1621-6.

Kjaer, Troels, Camilla Bertelsen, Paola Piccini, David Brooks, Jorgen Alving, and Hans Lou. "Increased Dopamine Tone during Meditation- Induced Change of Consciousness." Cognitive Brain Research 13, no. 2 (April 2002)

Kölmel HW. 1985. Complex visual hallucinations in the hemianopic field. J Neurol Neurosurg Psychiatry.

Koenig, Harold. "Research on Religion, Spirituality, and Mental Health: A Review." Canadian Journal of Psychiatry 54, no. 5 (May 2009)

Koenig, Harold, ed. Handbook of Religion and Mental Health. San Diego, CA: Academic Press, 1998

Kraepelin E. Psychiatry: A Textbook for Students and Physicians. New York, NY: Science History Publications; 1990.

Lauglin, Charles, John McManus, and Eugene d'Aquili. Brain, Symbol, and Experience. 2nd ed. New York: Columbia University Press, 1992

Lakoff, G. and M. Johnson (1999). Philosophy in the flesh. Basic Books: New York.

LeDoux, J. E. (1996). The emotional brain. New York: Simon & Schuster.

LeDoux, J.E. (1992), 'Emotion and the amygdala', in The Amygdala: Neurobiological Aspects of Emo- tion, Memory and Mental Dysfunction, ed J.P. Aggleton (New York: Wiley-Liss).

Levin, D.T. and Simons, D.J. (1997) Failure to detect changes to attended objects in motion pictures. Psychonomic Bulletin and Review 4, 501-6.

Levine,J. (1983) Materialism and qualia: the explanatory gap. Pacific Philosophical Quarterly 64, 354-61.

Levine,J. (2001) Purple Haze: The Puzzle of Consciousness. New York, Oxford University Press. Levine, S. (1979) A Gradual Awakening. New York, Doubleday.

Levinson, B.W. (1965) States of awareness during general anaesthesia. British Journal of Anaesthesia 37, 544-6.

Lewicki, P., Czyzewska, M. and Hoffman, H. (1987) Unconscious acquisition of complex procedural knowledge. Journal of Experimental Psychology: Learning, Memory and Cognition 13, 523-30.

Naskar, Abhijit. "What is Mind?", 2016

Naskar, Abhijit. "Love, God & Neurons: Memoir of A Scientist who found himself by getting lost", 2016

Naskar, Abhijit. "Principia Humanitas", 2017

Naskar, Abhijit. "We Are All Black: A Treatise on Racism", 2017

Naskar, Abhijit. "Either Civilized or Phobic: A Treatise on Homosexuality", 2017

Naskar, Abhijit. "Build Bridges not Walls: In the name of Americana", 2018

Naskar, Abhijit. "Citizens of Peace: Beyond the Savagery of Sovereignty", 2019

Naskar, Abhijit. "The Constitution of The United Peoples of Earth", 2019

Naskar, Abhijit. "Mission Reality", 2019

Naskar, Abhijit. "Good Scientist: When Science and Service Combine", 2020

Newberg, Andrew, and Jeremy Iversen. "The Neural Basis of the Complex Mental Task of Meditation: Neurotransmitter and Neurochemical Considerations." Medical Hypotheses 61, no. 2 (2003).

Newberg, Andrew. "How God Changes Your Brain: An Introduction to Jewish Neurotheology", CCAR

Journal: The Reform Jewish Quarterly, Winter 2016.

Newberg, Andrew, and Stephanie Newberg. "A Neuropsychological Perspective on Spiritual Development." In Handbook of Spiritual Development in Childhood and Adolescence, edited by Eugene Roehlkepartain, Pamela King, Linda Wagener, and Peter Benson. London: Sage Publications, Inc., 2005

Newberg, Andrew. "The Neurotheology Link An Intersection Between Spirituality and Health", Alternative and Complimentary Therapies, Vol 21 No 1, February 2015.

Newberg, Andrew, Nancy Wintering, Dharma Khalsa, Hannah Roggenkamp, and Mark Waldman. "Meditation Effects on Cognitive Function and Cerebral Blood Flow in Subjects with Memory Loss: A Preliminary Study." Journal of Alzheimer's Disease 20, no. 2 (2010)

Nash, M. (1995), 'Glimpses of the mind', Time.

Nesse RM. Proximate and evolutionary studies of anxiety, stress and depression: synergy at the interface. Neurosci Biobehav Rev. 1999;23:895-903.

Nicolelis, Miguel. (2011) "Beyond Boundaries: The New Neuroscience of Connecting Brains with Machines---and How It Will Change Our Lives", Times Books

O'Hara, K. and Scutt, T. (1996) There is no hard problem of consciousness. Journal of Consciousness Studies 3(4), 290-302, reprinted in J. Shear (ed.) (1997) Explaining Consciousness. Cambridge, MA, MIT Press, 69-82.

O'Regan, J.K. and Noe, A. (2001) A sensorimotor account of vision and visual consciousness. Behavioral and Brain Sciences 24(5), 883-917.

Ornstein, R.E. (1977) The Psychology of Consciousness (2nd edn). New York, Harcourt.

Ornstein, R.E. (1986) The Psychology of Consciousness (3rd edn). New York, Pehguin.

Ornstein, R.E. (1992) The Evolution of Consciousness. New York, Touchstone.

Penfield W, Faulk ME (1955) The insula: further observations on its function. Brain 78: 445– 470.

Penrose, R. (1994), Shadows of the Mind (Oxford: Oxford University Press).

Penrose, R. (1989), The Emperor's New Mind: Concerning Computers, Minds and The Laws of Physics (Oxford: Oxford University Press).

Persinger, "'I would kill in God's name' role of sex, weekly church attendance, report of a religious experience and limbic lability" Perceptual and Motor Skills 1997.

Persinger "Experimental simulation of the God experience" Neurotheology 2003.

Persinger, Corradini, Clement, Keaney, et al "Neurotheology and its convergence with neuroquantology" NeuroQuantology 2010.

Persinger. "The neuropsychiatry of paranormal experiences". J Neuropsychiatry Clin Neurosci 2001.

Persinger. "Neuropsychological bases of god beliefs", New York: Praeger, 1987

Persinger. "Temporal lobe epileptic signs and correlative behaviors displayed by normal populations", Journal of General Psychology, 1986

Perry BD, Pollard R. Homeostasis, stress, trauma, and adaptation. A neurodevelopmental view of childhood trauma. Child Adolesc Psychiatr Clin N Am. 1998;7:33.

Ramachandran VS. Behavioral and magnetoencephalographic correlates of plasticity in the adult human brain. Proc Natl Acad Sci USA 1993; 90: 10413–20.

Ramachandran VS. Plasticity and functional recovery in neurology. Clin Med 2005; 5: 368–73.

Rock I, Victor J. Vision and touch: an experimentally created conflict between the two senses. Science 1964; 143: 594–6.

Roberts, TA; Smalley, J; Ahrendt, D (December 2020). "Effect of gender affirming hormones on athletic performance in transwomen and transmen: implications for sporting organisations and legislators". British Journal of Sports Medicine. 55 (11): 577–583

Royet JP, Plailly J, Delon-Martin C, Kareken DA, Segebarth C (2003) fMRI of emotional responses to odors: influence of hedonic valence and judgment, handedness, and gender. Neuroimage 20: 713–728.

Rozin R Haidt J and McCauley CR (2000) Disgust. In: Lewis M, Haviland-Jones JM (eds) Handbook of Emotion. 2nd Edition. Guilford Press, New York, pp 637–653.

Saxe R, Carey S, Kanwisher N (2004) Understanding other minds: linking developmental psychology and functional neuroimaging. Annu Rev Psychol 55: 87–124.

S. J. Russell and P. Norvig, Artificial intelligence: a modern approach (3rd edition): Prentice Hall, 2009.

Singer T, Seymour B, O'Doherty J, Kaube H, Dolan RJ, Frith CD (2004) Empathy for pain involves the affective but not the sensory components of pain. Science 303: 1157–1162.

Smith A (1759) The theory of moral sentiments (ed. 1976). Clarendon Press, Oxford.

Schilling, Vincent. 2017, indian country today

Stein, Stephen K. 2017, The Sea in World History: Exploration, Travel, and Trade

Tesla N. "My Inventions", 1919

T. R. Society, "Machine learning: the power and promise of computers that learn by example," ed. The Royal Society, 2017.

Tomasello M, Call J (1997) Primate cognition. Oxford University Press, Oxford